Dedication

To my wife Nancy, son David,
married daughters Mary and Sarah,
acquired sons John and Chris, and
our precious granddaughters, Libby and Kate,

May we be ever mindful of God's gift of family
and the precious gift we each are to the other.

Acknowledgements

Any new work is often little more than a unique merging of the thoughts and ideas of others. As on an artists palette, hues and tones can be blended together in a distinctive way that gives rise to new perspectives and insights. The work you hold in your hands is no exception. It comes wrapped in appreciation and tied with a bow of gratitude for the hues and tones each of the following contributed to the rediscovery of this remarkable story of persistent faith in a faithful God:

- Bill Bullard, long-time friend and mentor who first modeled for me a passion and love for teaching the Scripture,

- Rev. Mark Slomka who first inspired what became an extended effort to further unfold the inspirational faith story of Zechariah and Elizabeth,

- Dr. James C. Martin of Bible World Seminars who first introduced me to the whole idea of Biblical context while walking the land with him in Israel,

- Dr. David Allen, a gifted teaching colleague, who infused me with the pastoral implications of his "Bermuda Triangle of the Soul,"[1]

- Camilla Seabolt and Pat Robertson of Community Bible Study who graciously asked me to share insights into Zechariah and Elizabeth's journey at their 2003 Teaching Directors' Conference,

- Dr. Sharon Bordine who kept encouraging me to connect the contextual dots and tell the larger story, and to Bruce Bordine who similarly kept encouraging me to keep on keeping on,

- Dr. D. Michael Crow and Dr. Bill and Dr. Marsha Nickels who repeatedly provided helpful editing as well as timely encouragement,

- My wife Nancy, whose patience and understanding allowed me to become immersed in contextually restoring Luke's narratives and who has faithfully accompanied me on our own version of this story, and

- Our son David, who has not only shaped a large part of our own faith journey, but who continues to both challenge and inspire us to persist in trusting in God's timing and ways *(see "Personal Reasons", Appendix)*.

Table of Contents

An Invitation

J esus and the writers of the Gospels were master storytellers. Their narratives were engaging and compelling stories that were rich and full of meaning to those who first heard them. *Zechariah and Elizabeth, Persistent Faith in a Faithful God* is a more expansive retelling of Luke's opening story *(see Appendix for full text.)* It uses the facts he provides and reconstructs the assumed context as Luke's original audience would have understood it.

The premise of this book is that context matters when we encounter the inspired words of Scripture. Furthermore, if we are to fully connect with the intended meaning of a passage today, we need to know what it meant to those who first heard those words. Restoring this essential context allows us to put ourselves into the mindset of the life and times of Zechariah and Elizabeth, and to experience their issues as if we were their neighbors. For a fuller development of this contextual approach, see *"The Case for Context"* in the Appendix.

The story of Zechariah and Elizabeth is not just a story. It was their reality, and a compelling journey of faith. When we understand it in context, we experience this couple's high hopes, faithful waiting, unfulfilled longings, painful misunderstandings and dashed dreams, which God ultimately restores in a most remarkable way. Through it all, Zechariah and Elizabeth persist in their faithfulness to God, trusting in Him as a God who remembers. As a result, their journey, with its waiting, wondering and resignation, as well as its challenge and comfort, speaks intimately to our own faith journeys in God's providential hand. At its core, their story is an awesome story about the wonders, surprises and faithfulness of our God who indeed remembers.

You will find appropriate *"Reflections to Share, Journal and Ponder"* for each chapter beginning on page 45. They can serve as guided discussion questions for small groups and Bible studies in a seven-week format as suggested in the Appendix. They can also guide personal meditation and journaling for devotional purposes.

So come and (re)discover Zechariah and Elizabeth—in their context. Let their persistently faithful journey in God's surprising providence stir and soothe your soul, as well as strengthen your willingness to trust Him, no matter what comes your way. ■

1

A Priest is Born

While Luke writes in shorthand, the message he pens is a full one. In a few introductory verses in Chapter 1, Luke has much to say as he sets the stage for the birth of Jesus and the unfolding of God's eternal plan of salvation. To wholly appreciate his opening narrative, we must journey back through the story of Zechariah and Elizabeth—real people dealing with the real issues of life—as if we had the mindset of first century Middle Eastern villagers.

In the time of Herod king of Judea... (5a)

Luke opens his historical narrative by informing us that Herod the Great was in power, a bitter reminder that Rome occupies the land. To a devout Jew, this was a dark and oppressive time; Roman occupation was viewed as the equivalent of the kingdom of evil ruling the land.

Herod is also the rebuilder and political controller of the great Temple in Jerusalem. The mention of his name is a reminder that the current Temple high priesthood, who hold their Temple "franchise" subject to Herod's continuing approval[2], are not only illegitimate[3], but corrupt. Thus, Luke is reminding us that there is a spiritual vacuum in those controlling the land and the Temple. Because of this, many Jews were prayerfully waiting for God to change the leadership over both. As they intensely prayed for that outcome, many would have remembered God's covenant with David,[4] that there would come a time when He would send One to establish a new authority in the land and a new spirit of worship in the Temple. That is part of the backdrop that Luke assumes we realize as he starts to unfold this story.

there was a priest named Zechariah... (5b)

Other than the issues associated with Rome's oppression and the spiritual sterility of Temple leadership, we know little about the events, circumstances or issues surrounding Zechariah's birth.

Nothing indicates why his father gave him that name. However, based on the significance of naming in that culture, we can infer that Zechariah's birth was felt by his father to be a meaningful response by God to something very significant in his life. So let's go back to the beginning of this story.

Zechariah's father, an ordinary Levitical priest whose name we do not know, had just heard his baby's first cry. As he waited outside the room where his wife had struggled to give birth, perhaps he wondered if Jehovah had blessed him with a child who could carry on the priestly tradition of the family. When he learned he had a son, he was overwhelmed with joy, gratitude and perhaps even a sense of fulfillment.

As the infant's father looked out over the land, his discouragement from Rome's oppression and the compromise of Temple worship may well have filled his soul with longings for Messiah. For both personal reasons, as well as national concerns, he could start to sense an appropriate name for this newborn son. And so when the eighth day came, the time for circumcision and the naming of this blessed gift from the Lord, this righteous priest declared the infant's name to be *Zechariah*. Because the Semitic meaning of Zechariah is "whom Jehovah remembers,"[5] his son now had a name that invokes the personal, covenantal name of God, and recalls His promises and testimony to be faithful to his people.[6] During a desperate time for the nation, Zechariah was a name that combined his father's plea and solemn prayer of faith together with his sense of celebration for the birth of this son.

In choosing this name, Zechariah's father drew upon a prophetic name that harkens back almost 500 years in the nation's history. In the time of returning from Babylon to rebuild the Temple, a prophet and priest named Zechariah was visited by an angel. From that vision, he penned God's words of prophetic hope that promised a "restored kingdom community and a functioning temple."[7] The mention of Zechariah's name evokes prophetic echoes of Messiah's coming, priesthood, kingship, glory and His enduring reign of peace and prosperity. Those words from long ago also served as another reminder of the covenantal promise that God made to David.

In a culture in which the act of naming was highly significant and naming a male child a most sacred and solemn task, Zechariah's father had just given him a name that came with a history and a legacy. He would now journey through the rest of his days never forgetting what the Lord had done for his father, as well as his father's (and the nation's) hopes for the land and the Temple. He would always remember how his father had memorialized those intense longings and desires with his name.

Growing up, Zechariah probably heard his father recount the significance of his name until he could recite that history backward and forward in his sleep. "Whom Jehovah remembers" would have been ingrained in his mind and embossed on his soul. Its legacy would be an imprint on his character that he could never forget, never deny, never walk away from: "The Lord God of Abraham, Isaac and Jacob always remembers, and had remembered his father too. And my name signifies all that, and more!" ■

For "Reflections to Share, Journal and Ponder," see page 45.

2

Great Expectations

...his wife Elizabeth was also a descendant of Aaron... (5c)

Having been blessed and entrusted by God with this son, Zechariah's father had other cultural responsibilities. One of these was to arrange his son's marriage, which could not be with just any family from the tribes of Israel. If priests wanted their sons to remain in the priesthood, their sons had to marry the daughters of priests.[8] And because Zechariah's birth seemed to be so significant, his father may have wondered if he could arrange for a very special wife.

Finally a family with a daughter was found for a possible marriage that seemed almost too good to be true. The daughter was named Elizabeth, the name of Aaron's wife[9]. Because Aaron had been Israel's very first Chief Priest, and with Elizabeth's name meaning "one who swears by God,"[10] if one wanted a great name and legacy for a priest's wife, this was it!

When the marriage details were agreed to, and the betrothal contract between the two families finalized, Zechariah's father was overjoyed. His son had married into Aaron's priestly line, just as his father had, and generations of their fathers before him. In the eyes of this culture, this marriage was now official even though the wedding ceremony would not take place for nearly a year.

Once again, Zechariah's father might have mused, "Yes indeed, I certainly did give him the right name! With this marriage, the Lord has truly remembered both me and my son." Perhaps he continued to wonder, "Maybe the Lord has something truly wonderful in store for his young priest-to-be and his seemingly special wife. Perhaps there might also be something very special about their family," he thought. "Of course there will be a family," he told himself. "Everyone knows that one of God's first commands was to 'Be fruitful and increase in number.'[11]

The only question is how many children, and more particularly, how many priestly sons might God bless them with? Might one of their sons carry on the prophetic tradition embodied in the legacy of Zechariah's name? Yes, it will be a wonderful wedding and a most joyous occasion."

When the time came for the wedding feast and the consummation of the marriage, Zechariah was at least twenty years old and Elizabeth most likely around thirteen.[12] Intertwined with the joy of this event were high hopes and dreams for this couple and their marriage. In this religious culture, children were seen as God's direct and evident blessing to His people.[13] Everyone knew that the giving of life was God's prerogative. However, if God looked with disfavor on you, you would have no children as punishment for your guilt.[14] For most people, there was no ambiguity in this way of thinking. Either God looked upon you with favor, or He didn't. You were either "righteous" or you were a "sinner." You were either "in" or "out." Even the Lord's disciples were later to reflect this commonly held perspective.[15] Therefore, it is no surprise that in this culture "barrenness was a woman's and a family's greatest misfortune."[16]

As Zechariah and Elizabeth ended their wedding festivities, and had a moment to contemplate what their life together might be, they could never have envisioned how the coming decades would unfold. They, like we, would have had their own expectations of how they thought their family life should be. And in defining their expectations for a family, they unknowingly set the stage for future disappointment.

Both of them were upright in the sight of God, observing all the Lord's commandments and regulations blamelessly. (6)

Luke informs us that Zechariah and Elizabeth were upright ("righteous" in several other translations) in God's eyes. In this culture, that meant that they were behaviorally obedient in observing the Ten Commandments, as well as all the Levitical laws concerning diet, including all the feasts and festivals. In describing Zechariah and Elizabeth this way, Luke is also telling us that God looked upon this couple with favor, not only because of their faithful behavior, but because their hearts were right in God's sight as well.

Luke's use of the present tense "observing" ("walking blamelessly" in the NASB) tells us that this couple consistently lived out this righteous posture toward God. So far, in the mindset of Luke's first-century readers, there is nothing unusual or unexpected in the unfolding of this story. So far it all fits with their understanding of how things work for "good" people. ■

For "Reflections to Share, Journal and Ponder," see page 46.

3

Waiting

... who belonged to the priestly division of Abijah... (5c)

By this time in Israel's history, the number of ordinary Levitical priests is estimated to be upwards of 20,000.[17] For organizational purposes, the priesthood was divided into 24 divisions[18] of approximately 850 priests each. Each division was further separated into six family branches, or clans.[19] Through rotating the Temple work among these 24 divisions, each division would be on duty for one week's service, then off for 23 weeks while the other priestly divisions served in their appointed order. While on duty, each of the family clans served for one day with all six clans joining together to serve on the Sabbath.[20]

One of the obligations of each division's service was performing the four mandated daily offerings and sacrifices. This included the incense offering in the Holy Place which, because of its location so close to the Holy of Holies, [21] was considered to be the most coveted service for a priest to carry out. Since there were generally more priests in a division than might ever be able to perform the incense offering, a priest was allowed to serve once in his lifetime.[22] As a result, a lot-casting system was established to allow God to select the priest He desired to honor with that service.

The lot-casting procedure was well prescribed.[23] Those priests who had not been previously chosen in the family clan for this service would gather prior to the incense offering in the Chamber of Hewn Stone,[24] located in Temple Mount. There they would position themselves in a circle with the leader of the family clan at the center. After required prayers, the leader approached a priest of his choosing in the circle and removed his headdress (turban). This act indicated where the lot counting would begin. As the headdress was being lifted, each of the priests in the circle simultaneously raised a hand in front of himself, pointing one finger upwards.[25]

The leader would then announce a self-selected number significantly greater than the number of priests in the circle,[26] such as 187. The process of counting fingers would then start from one to 187, beginning with the priest whose headdress had been removed. Counting progressed around the circle from priest to priest until 187 fingers were numbered. The priest with the 187th finger was the one selected from the family clan to perform the incense offering that day. After decades of participating in this process (some consider Zechariah to be sixty years old when Luke introduces us to him[27]), Zechariah never gets selected. Sometimes the count ended just before him, and sometimes just after, but never with him.

> *Both of them were upright in the sight of God, observing all the Lord's commandments and regulations blamelessly. But they had no child, because Elizabeth was barren, and they were both well along in years. (6–7)*

With incredible economy of words, and with sudden, new and unexpected information, Luke packs decades of pain, disappointment, hurt, frustration, self-doubt and misunderstanding into one sentence, with the word "barren" being the most arresting. In doing so, Luke quickly introduces an inconceivable fact into the minds of his first-century readers. What he now reveals just doesn't make sense with the way their religious world was thought to work. To be considered upright in God's eyes, and yet to be barren all these years, was incomprehensible to Luke's listeners. It was outside a devout Jew's mindset, it simply could not be. Something was wrong with this picture. In Zechariah and Elizabeth's culture, God didn't bless "righteous" people that way. Everybody knows that—or do they?

As the decades unfolded, two things were undisputedly clear. Zechariah and Elizabeth were childless, and Zechariah was never chosen for incense offering service. Statistically speaking, there may well have been some younger priests in the clan who were childless, and also a few other priests who had sons, but who had not yet been chosen for incense service. But it is highly improbable that there were any other priests in the family clan who were childless, never selected for the incense offering and also as old as Zechariah.

Since the community's religious mindset could not accept the contradictory realities of being barren and never selected with also being righteous, one factor had to be dismissed. Therefore, only one conclusion was possible within the family clan's mindset. Although Zechariah and Elizabeth appeared to be righteous, they must have offended God in some way, and He is punishing them for their sin. ■

For "Reflections to Share, Journal and Ponder," see page 47.

4

Being Misunderstood

...taken away my disgrace among the people. (25b)

In walking to and from the Temple all those years, Zechariah may have reflected many times on the implications of his name, one "whom Jehovah remembers," and the context in which his father gave it to him. Every time Zechariah came to Jerusalem, he saw Roman soldiers standing guard around the Temple and wondered, "How long must the nation wait?" And whenever he thought about Elizabeth, he wondered how long must the two of them wait. What if they never had a child? Was Jehovah remembering him, or might the Lord have passed them by?

Zechariah's return to the Temple every 24 weeks must have felt more and more uncomfortable to him, even embarrassing. With each passing year, he still had not been chosen for the incense offering. And with each passing year, fewer priests from his era remained in the circle. At the same time, more of their sons stood in their places, appearing ever younger to the aging Zechariah. Finally, it may have reached the point where Zechariah was the conspicuous old man of the lot-casting process, ever more prominent as the "passed over" priest.

During this time Elizabeth never became pregnant. Might Zechariah have wondered what the other priests in his clan were thinking about this? Was there unspoken judgment from his family branch? One can imagine some of the whisperings, "That Zechariah thinks he's righteous, but we know better. If he and Elizabeth were as righteous as they pretend, surely they would have had children by now." Might this atmosphere have reinforced Zechariah's feeling that God may have indeed forgotten them?

Our religious mindsets, those frameworks in which we think, process and make judgments, can so easily inflict pain in the lives of those who do not conform to our understanding of how things should be. When Elizabeth would walk to the village well to draw water, those painful arrows of misunderstanding from her peers may well have pierced her soul. Year after year, her sense of inadequacy grew. After all, procreation was her God-given task. Her identity, purpose, and meaning were—as were any Jewish woman's at that time—largely involved in fulfilling that role. Over the decades, the social rejection and cultural humiliation Elizabeth felt within the extended family may well have coalesced into a deep sense of perpetual shame.[28] In her own words, Elizabeth acknowledges "my disgrace among the people." J.B. Phillips, in his Modern English Bible, translates Elizabeth's words as "the shame that I have suffered." Not only did she live with a chronic sense of feeling misunderstood, but most likely experienced a corresponding sense of powerlessness, realizing there was nothing she could do about it.

Put yourself in Zechariah and Elizabeth's sandals for a moment. You're doing right in God's eyes, but your religious culture says you *must* be doing something wrong! This implicit and progressive religious disapproval of Zechariah and Elizabeth's life didn't just suddenly happen. It occurred gradually and imperceptibly. "After all, it's not that unusual for conception to take some time," the culture would reason, as would Zechariah and Elizabeth. "We all know good people who waited years for their first-born." As reasonable as this rationale may be, in Zechariah and Elizabeth's case the cultural acceptability of their childlessness seemed to be stretched further with each passing year. Finally it was stretched to the breaking point of religious believability.

Sometimes life's heaviest burdens are rooted in unsolvable misunderstandings. And with each decade, misguided inferences from Zechariah and Elizabeth's religious culture gradually began to acquire the rigidity of explicit dogma. "We hold these truths to be self-evident," their culture would conclude, "these two are receiving God's disfavor for their secret sin!"[29] Reinforcing this dogmatic perspective was the teaching of some rabbis who held that there were only two conditions for which it could not be argued that God was chastening a person because He loved them: leprosy and childlessness.[30] We can only imagine how painful that perspective must have been to the psyche and souls of these two righteous Levites.

Moreover, when these painful projected-on-to-you messages come from your own extended family, they can cut even deeper into the fabric of your soul, making you feel very different, very misunderstood, very sad, and very much alone.

Luke gives us insight into how Zechariah and Elizabeth handled this progressive accumulation of cultural disgrace. They simply persevered in being faithful. Looking a few verses ahead, we get a glimpse into that reality when the angel informs Zechariah, "your petition has been heard." But how did the two of them persist in carrying on a faithful walk? Luke informs us that they prayed. Being righteous Jews meant that they prayed dozens of times daily in a very prescribed manner. Thus in their latter years, Zechariah and Elizabeth prayed even when they wondered what it all meant. They continued to pray even when their hearts were weary and heavy from waiting. No doubt they also prayed when they didn't feel like praying at all, especially when they felt they were now waiting in vain for a son. ■

For "Reflections to Share, Journal and Ponder," see page 48.

5

Unfulfilled Longings and God's Plan

Both of them were upright in the sight of God, observing all the Lord's commandments and regulations blamelessly. (6)

With each passing year, Israel had waited yet another year for Messiah to come. Likewise, Zechariah and Elizabeth waited yet another year for a child. Another series of attempts at conception had been followed by an equal number of obvious failures. And each failed outcome added to an already long list of failures. How frustrating! Year after year, decade after decade, each hopeful attempt was inevitably followed by even more disappointment.

How might years of waiting have affected this couple? What did they talk about during their meals? Did they ever share their cultural wounds and sorrows with each other? Did they discuss their disappointments about how life together seemed to have turned out so differently from what they had expected? Or did they keep these deep feelings to themselves?

There might have been times of soul-searching and self-doubt. "What are we doing wrong?" Zechariah and Elizabeth might have asked each other. "We must be missing something! How could we possibly be offending God? Why is barrenness still a part of our lives?" Luke gives us no clues that answers ever came to those questions. Yet, they remained faithful in walking blamelessly (present tense). In their decades of waiting, Zechariah and Elizabeth never allowed their shared sense of being "passed over" to degenerate into cynicism and despair. They never permitted their profound sense of unfulfilled longing and discouragement to paralyze them. And more than once after their monthly attempts at conception, Zechariah may have pondered the irony of his name, "whom God remembers.", questioning yet again, "Could it be that God has forgotten us?," All the while this couple's shared sense of unfulfilled longing for a child went deeper and deeper into the marrow of their souls. How long can a soul ache for something seemingly so right before it begins to lose its grip on hope?

While Zechariah and Elizabeth continued to faithfully wait without answers, God was at work at a higher level setting the earthly stage for the entry of His only begotten Son into the world. As part of this preparation, God was using the Roman Empire, with its years of internal wars finally over, to bring a civil peace to the known world for the very first time. As part of His ever-unfolding plan, God had also caused the Roman Empire to establish a standard language, Greek, as well as to develop the first worldwide road network. All of this was part of God's perfectly orchestrated "Word became flesh"[31] rescue and restoration plan for the world.[32]

For the first time in history, a sense of predictable physical safety freed people to think about spiritual things. Furthermore, there would now be a commonly understood language in place, as well as a road system that could be used to quickly disseminate important news to anywhere in the known world.[33] In God's plan, all of this needed to be in place before the birth of Jesus. Just thirty-three years later, God would use this Roman troika of civil peace, common language and worldwide road system to rapidly spread a new message: the Good News of the life-saving, life-changing sacrifice of Jesus the Messiah on Calvary's Cross.

The irony of all this is mind boggling. While the Jewish nation was chafing under Roman rule, with many praying for their concept of Messiah to come and deliver them, God was at work using the Roman Empire to prepare the earth for the coming of His Son. With the world's stage now set, the time had come for His humble birth in a small town, in a small country intentionally positioned at the crossroads of the world of antiquity. And to start to unfold the next phase of God's plan, the angel Gabriel was summoned and briefed for his visitation to an unassuming priest named Zechariah who faithfully served Jehovah in this land. ■

For "Reflections to Share, Journal and Ponder," see page 50.

6

Dashed Dreams

God's eternally conceived plan, which always included Zechariah and Elizabeth and their unanswered questions, continued to unfold unimpeded. This couple just didn't know it and couldn't see it. That's why they needed a persistent faith to go forward into each new day. While Zechariah and Elizabeth could not fathom God's plan, they continued to implicitly trust in Jehovah as a God who remembers. They rested in God's nature, His attributes, His faithfulness, even when their childlessness made no sense to them.

Eventually it became increasingly clear to both Zechariah and Elizabeth that conceiving a child was no longer a biological possibility. It seemed a forgone conclusion that there would never be a son to carry on Zechariah's priestly tradition. A biological point of no return had been reached, and there was no turning back the clock. What was it like at the dinner table during that time? Did either of them say anything to the other? Perhaps not. There are times when words just serve to devalue the profundity of a deeply intense emotional reality. There may have only been the internal sobbing in their respective souls as they each pondered their own desperate longings for a child who would now never be.

Perhaps, yet again, the irony of his name occurred to Zechariah. Could the Lord possibly be remembering their almost four-decade's journey as a couple and their continuing plight of childlessness? How does one persist in faith when there no longer seems to be any point to persisting? Luke tells us the couple prayed and observed all that God had commanded, just as they had always done, and with a heart that pleased Him. They simply kept on walking blamelessly before the Lord. Meanwhile, their shared unfulfilled longings for a child may well have stretched the yearnings of their hearts to the breaking point.

Their cumulative sadness was heavy, their home profoundly empty, and the silence to their question "why" was never louder. Yet they continued to persist in faithful waiting even when there seemed to be no good reason to wait any more. ■

For "Reflections to Share, Journal and Ponder," see page 52.

7

An Incredible Announcement

*Once when Zechariah's division was on duty and he was
serving as priest before God, He was chosen by lot, according
to the custom of the priesthood, to go into the temple of
the Lord and burn incense. (8-9)*

While on duty yet again with his Division and family clan, and perhaps now approaching his fourth decade of service in the priesthood, Zechariah was finally chosen by lot to perform the coveted incense offering. At last, he would enter the Holy Place in the Temple to perform this offering at the Altar of Incense. Given the design of that part of the Temple, he would now be within thirty feet of the Ark of the Covenant in the Holy of Holies, separated only by the massive veil that divided these two chambers.[34] For one who might have thought he was overlooked, or even forgotten by God, Zechariah would now be as close to the Presence of God as anyone but the High Priest could ever be!

Zechariah's sudden, surprising selection might well have evoked some conflicting emotions. Perhaps he said to himself,

"Can this be?"

"Is this a mistake?"

"Why now?"

Or even "Woe is me!"

Perhaps his priestly peers had similar thoughts. After all these years, especially given Elizabeth's long barrenness, what could this mean? Might this be the validation of something? But of what? Could this be ominous? In Temple worship tradition, the upwards trail of incense smoke was viewed as signifying the ascending prayers of the people rising up to God.[35] That understanding might have prompted Zechariah to consider raising his prayer for a son one more (maybe last) time as he was praying while prostrate in the Holy Place.

Then an angel of the Lord appeared to him, standing at the
right side of the altar of incense. When Zechariah saw him,
he was startled and was gripped with fear. (11–12)

For a brief moment, if Zechariah recalled the demise of Aaron's
sons in the presence of the Lord,[36] he might have thought that "Woe
is me!" was the best response. "Somehow", he might have reasoned,
"my wife and I must have been displeasing God, and now I am going
to find out why and face our judgment. At least we will finally know,
after all these years, what we have been doing to displease the Lord."
But, if Zechariah could have thought more clearly for just a
moment, this surprise visit might well have heartened him. With
this angelic visitation, Jehovah obviously had not forgotten him!

Then an angel of the Lord appeared to him, standing at the
right side of the altar of incense. When Zechariah saw him, he
was startled and was gripped with fear. But the angel said
to him: "Do not be afraid, Zechariah; your prayer has been
heard. Your wife Elizabeth will bear you a son, and you are to
give him the name John. He will be a joy and delight to you, and
many will rejoice because of his birth, for he will be great in the
sight of the Lord. He is never to take wine or other fermented
drink, and he will be filled with the Holy Spirit even from
birth. Many of the people of Israel will he bring back to the
Lord their God. And he will go on before the Lord, in the
spirit and power of Elijah, to turn the hearts of the fathers to their
children and the disobedient to the wisdom of the righteous—to
make ready a people prepared for the Lord. (13–17)

With these words, Zechariah is informed he will be the father
of a son and that this son will prepare the way for Messiah! It is
hard to imagine what might have been going on in his mind and
emotions as he heard these words from the angel. Furthermore, this
was going to be an extraordinary son, great in the sight of the Lord.
This son will prophetically "turn the hearts"[37] of people, bringing
repentance to many in Israel. In so doing, he and Elizabeth would
make people ready for Messiah. All the significance of Zechariah's
name will now be coming to fruition. Messiah is coming and he
will have a son. But did Zechariah really hear those words? Did he
really hear what he had just been told? Apparently not.

Zechariah asked the angel, "How can I be sure of this? I
am an old man and my wife is well along in years." (18)

Zechariah is honored by God to be the first person to learn that the Messiah's coming is imminent. Yet his initial response has to do with biological issues! Nor can he even trust the Lord's promise of a son, which suggests that perhaps he had prayed his ascending prayers without any conviction they would be answered. While Zechariah has long been faithful, he is not perfect, nor can he be expected to be. This momentary expression of doubt and disbelief does not change him into a faithless priest.

Not unlike us, Zechariah was so focused on the unfulfilled longings of his heart that he couldn't hear the fullness of God's message—the incredible "good news" that Messiah is coming! This is the one announcement that the nation of Israel has been longing and waiting to hear for centuries. Luke's readers must have wondered what God's response would be to Zechariah's physiological preoccupation and resultant disbelief. As will shortly become clear, in this particular setting the expression of doubt and disbelief does have its consequences.

> *The angel answered, "I am Gabriel. I stand in the presence of God, and I have been sent to speak to you and to tell you this good news. And now you will be silent and not able to speak until the day this happens, because you did not believe my words, which will come true at their proper time." Meanwhile, the people were waiting for Zechariah and wondering why he stayed so long in the temple. When he came out, he could not speak to them. They realized he had seen a vision in the temple, for he kept making signs to them but remained unable to speak. (19–22)*

Part of the protocol of the incense offering was for the officiating priest to pronounce the prescribed Numbers 6:24-26 blessing at the end of the liturgy.[38] What the people always heard at the end of that service was the officiating priest with uplifted hands pronounce,

> *Jehovah bless thee, and keep thee: Jehovah make His face shine upon thee: And be gracious unto thee: Jehovah lift up His countenance upon thee and Give thee peace.*

To this the people would always respond,[39]

> *Blessed be the Lord God, the God of Israel, from everlasting to everlasting.*

When it came time for Zechariah to say this blessing, he opened his mouth and nothing came out! As far as we know, this was the only time the blessing at the end of the incense offering could not be uttered by the officiating priest. Talk about instant notoriety. Suddenly this oft-passed-over priest is the "talk of the Temple," and this news will soon travel back to his own village.

Silence is often God's prescription for those times when we are having difficulty listening to Him, when we are so preoccupied with our own issues that we don't hear, or can't take time to listen to God's "still small voice." God, who designed and made us, knows what we need to live abundantly so as to honor Him. As our Creator, He knows we need periods of solitude and silence to reflect, to listen, to regain our perspective, to refocus on who He is, His will and His ways. God is perfectly aware of all that Zechariah is and what his realities are. God does "remember" Zechariah and blesses him with silence as well as a son, the significance of which Zechariah cannot yet comprehend. As part of His grace and restorative discipline, God gives Zechariah an opportunity to reflect and refocus.

Going home, Zechariah now has a new challenge. Now mute, and considered by his culture to be possibly deaf as well,[40] he cannot easily communicate. How will he explain all this to Elizabeth? For starters, Zechariah now needs to find a writing tablet so he can share this incredible experience with her.

When Zechariah, mute, walked back into their home in Judea, Elizabeth realized something profound had happened. But what? Slowly Zechariah told the story in a way that Elizabeth could understand. As part of this process, there had to be a marvelous moment when Elizabeth finally recognized the significance of what the angel had said to Zechariah. They were going to have a son! Then there followed another wonderful moment, when Zechariah wrote on his tablet that they needed to be intimate one more time. This time there would be no failure and disappointment. What a poignant and healing moment that must have been for the two of them. ■

For "Reflections to Share, Journal and Ponder," see page 53.

8

Restoration

"The Lord has done this for me," she said. "In these days he has shown his favor and taken away my disgrace among the people." (25)

God has his ways and they are very different from ours. Although Zechariah is mute in silence, what happened to him in the Temple is now a matter of much public discussion. Elizabeth is now pregnant and in several months will be openly acknowledging and sharing news of God's womb-opening grace. The shame of many years is suddenly and dramatically gone. Her unfulfilled longings have finally been fulfilled. Decades of waiting have become God's "fullness of time" for them. Yes, God has His surprising ways.

Elizabeth has now been rescued from her seemingly ever-present struggle with cultural humiliation and social rejection. "Nothing is impossible with God" will become a recurrent theme of her heart. Her son will prepare the way for the Lord's Messiah. And as part of the unfolding of that plan, Zechariah and Elizabeth have been dramatically rescued. Yes, God does indeed have His ways. He does remember!

In Luke's compelling narrative, not only does the Lord remember this couple, He rescues them. In so doing, He honors their decades of righteous waiting. In the process of being released from her cultural disgrace, Elizabeth is restored to social acceptance in a most significant way. In opening her womb, God has not only taken away her disgrace, but has also lifted her up to an honored position in the family clan. She has gone from being on the "outs" to being very "in," from being marginalized and excluded, to being at the epicenter of inclusion. What a reversal! That is often God's way.

Because of Zechariah's Holy Place visitation, it is now clear to many in the clan that someone special is growing in Elizabeth's womb. For years to come, people will be talking about her son's birth announcement, and later his adult, "preparing the way" ministry.

What Elizabeth can't see is that her priestly son will become the greatest of the prophets[41], carrying on the prophetic tradition of Zechariah's name in a most remarkable way. Elizabeth has become, and will be for the rest of her days, a very special person in the eyes of her greater family and culture. She experiences God's restoration in a most remarkable way. Yes, the Lord rescues. Yes,the Lord restores. God has His ways. And, yes, the Lord certainly does remember! ■

For "Reflections to Share, Journal and Ponder" see page 54.

9

God's Gracious Glimpse

In the sixth month, God sent the angel Gabriel to Nazareth, a town in Galilee, to a virgin pledged to be married to a man named Joseph, a descendant of David. The virgin's name was Mary. The angel went to her and said, "Greetings, you who are highly favored! The Lord is with you." Mary was greatly troubled at his words and wondered what kind of greeting this might be. But the angel said to her, "Do not be afraid, Mary, you have found favor with God. You will be with child and give birth to a son, and you are to give him the name Jesus. He will be great and will be called the Son of the Most High. The Lord God will give him the throne of his father David, and he will reign over the house of Jacob forever; his kingdom will never end." "How will this be," Mary asked the angel, "since I am a virgin?" The angel answered, "The Holy Spirit will come upon you, and the power of the Most High will overshadow you. So the holy one to be born will be called the Son of God. Even Elizabeth your relative is going to have a child in her old age, and she who was said to be barren is in her sixth month. For nothing is impossible with God." "I am the Lord's servant," Mary answered. "May it be to me as you have said." Then the angel left her. (26–38)

L uke suddenly shifts his narrative focus from Judea in the south to Galilee in the north, from senior citizen Elizabeth to a (most likely) twelve-and-one-half year old girl named Mary. As Luke continues to unfold his narrative, he contrasts two wombs: one long closed and another never opened, two wombs always intended to be intertwined in God's eternal plan.

The message that the angel brought Mary was not initially "good news" at all. From Mary's cultural perspective, becoming pregnant while betrothed could, at worst, result in death by stoning for adultery.[42] Best case would be a lifelong stigma that would prevent her from ever marrying. Aware of how things worked in that culture, Mary instantly knew all her hopes and dreams for an ordinary and uneventful life were gone. In her worldview, the most likely thing to happen now would be for Joseph to go back to the scribe and undo the betrothal contract with a writ of divorce. As a result, Mary would never have a husband, and therefore no "social security" for the rest of her days. Furthermore, in the devoutly religious culture of Nazareth, her son would forever be known as the illegitimate son of Mary.[43] In one moment, this pre-pubescent unassuming girl knew her life had been dramatically changed forever.

Knowing that these perceptions would be part of Mary's social and cultural reality, God encourages Mary in this bewildering and deeply perplexing moment. He has the angel inform Mary that Elizabeth, her relative, is with child. Elizabeth now becomes the case history that God uses to encourage Mary in the midst of all this overwhelmingly heavy news. Being a relative, most likely a cousin, Mary would have known of Elizabeth's plight and years of disgrace. Therefore she may have immediately understood the significance of Elizabeth's pregnancy as miraculous. And just to make sure the meaning of Elizabeth's newly opened womb is not lost on Mary (remember Zechariah heard, but didn't truly listen), God has the angel declare to Mary, "For nothing is impossible with God." To Mary, suddenly beginning to realize the inherent shame of her new situation, this gracious glimpse into Elizabeth's new reality must have been a great encouragement.

What was the impact of Elizabeth's newly announced pregnancy upon Mary? Luke's next verse provides insight. Mary replies in a spirit of submission and faith to the angel by declaring, "I am the Lord's servant...may it be to me as you have said." With her response, Luke portrays Mary as the measuring stick for a disciple. At the same time, Luke gives us a deeply practical insight into the nature of Mary's faith. With Mary, faith is not just an intellectual proposition, but a verb lived out in submission to God's will and ways. She lives out her faith even when every cultural fiber of her being tells her that this may never be in her best interest.

Elizabeth's faith history is now Mary's faith-uplifting encouragement. It will help sustain Mary as she journeys forward into her new unknown. Elizabeth doesn't know any of this yet. But that did not keep God from using her faith journey to encourage Mary. Isn't God amazing! Isn't it wondrous how He works, and when? God indeed has His ways.

At that time Mary got ready and hurried to a town in the hill country of Judea, where she entered Zechariah's home and greeted Elizabeth. When Elizabeth heard Mary's greeting, the baby leaped in her womb, and Elizabeth was filled with the Holy Spirit. In a loud voice she exclaimed: "Blessed are you among women, and blessed is the child you will bear! But why am I so favored, that the mother of my Lord should come to me? As soon as the sound of your greeting reached my ears, the baby in my womb leaped for joy. Blessed is she who has believed that what the Lord has said to her will be accomplished!" (39–45)

In this anointed encounter of two women whose wombs are suddenly opening, some of the clouds of "why" questions now start to part for Elizabeth. She is now given a gracious glimpse into the question of barrenness that has long been a part of hers and Zechariah's lives. God gives her a new perspective by allowing her to look back through "the rear-view mirror" and get a glimpse of His grace. Elizabeth is now presented with the realization of why she and Zechariah had to wait all these years to become pregnant. They had to wait for Mary to be born, and then for her to come of childbearing age. Now, at long last, the pieces of their life puzzle start falling into place. Unlike many of our desires, their longings for a son were always rooted in God's plan for them. Now all of those years of being misunderstood, of feeling disgraced, of not knowing, are anointed with the beauty of God's purpose and meaning. It was a wonderfully restorative and healing glimpse into their "why" questions. Their decades of waiting with unfulfilled longings were intentional in God's hand. It served a purpose, a glorious purpose, His purpose. It revealed and displayed God's glory. He indeed has His ways!

Zechariah and Elizabeth's courage and life-long commitment to persist in their faith is now undergirded with an added realization. God was at work all that time; they just didn't know it and couldn't see it. Of course, they had to wait until Mary's "fullness of time" had come. They now begin to realize that God's "fullness of time" was converging for all three of them. Elizabeth's was a womb long closed; Mary's is a womb being opened. God was at work at a higher level, and with a higher purpose, than either could have ever imagined. Unaware of this, Zechariah and Elizabeth remained faithful, and Mary submits in faith. This is something Elizabeth observes and reinforces with her affirmation of Mary. What a marvelous moment it must have been for both of them! It fact it was so wonderful and so overwhelming for Mary that she bursts forth with a litany of praise that we have come to call her *Magnificat*.[44] Elizabeth had a role to play, directed by God, in helping to evoke this inspired worship as Mary responds to God in awe and wonder for who He is and how He does things. ■

For "Reflections to Share, Journal and Ponder" see page 55.

10

A New Priest is Born

When it was time for Elizabeth to have her baby, she gave birth to a son. Her neighbors and relatives heard that the Lord had shown her great mercy, and they shared her joy. On the eighth day they came to circumcise the child, and they were going to name him after his father Zechariah, but his mother spoke up and said, "No! He is to be called John." They said to her, "There is no one among your relatives who has that name." Then they made signs to his father, to find out what he would like to name the child. He asked for a writing tablet, and to everyone's astonishment he wrote, "His name is John." (57-63)

The weight of tradition in this culture suggests it would be most appropriate if Zechariah's newborn son should also be named Zechariah. Yet the friends and relatives offering this logical and well-intentioned advice knew nothing of God's purposes and His command to the child's father. "Zechariah would certainly be an obviously appropriate name for the Lord has indeed remembered him in a most remarkable way," they may have reasoned.

Yet God wants to reveal more of Himself by His choice of the name John, which means "God is gracious."[45] Yes, He certainly is a God who remembers *and* He is also an utterly faithful God who is wonderfully gracious, as the gift of His only Son to the world will eternally attest.

His father Zechariah was filled with the Holy Spirit and prophesied: "Praise be to the Lord, the God of Israel, because he has come and has redeemed his people. He has raised up a horn of salvation for us in the house of his servant David (as he said through his holy prophets of long ago), salvation from our enemies and from the hand of all who hate us to show mercy to our fathers and to remember his holy covenant, the oath he swore to our father Abraham: to rescue us from the hand of our enemies, and to enable us to serve him without

*fear in holiness and righteousness before him all our days.
And you, my child, will be called a prophet of the Most High;
for you will go on before the Lord to prepare the way for him,
to give his people the knowledge of salvation through the
forgiveness of their sins, because of the tender mercy of our
God, by which the rising sun will come to us from heaven to
shine on those living in darkness and in the shadow of death,
to guide our feet into the path of peace." And the child grew
and became strong in spirit; and he lived in the desert until
he appeared publicly to Israel. (67–80)*

Praising God is the soul's supernaturally inspired response to
His overwhelming grace and faithfulness. To worship is to respond
to Him. Filled to overflowing with praise and gratitude, Zechariah
responded to God for who He is and how He does things. Having
memorized the Torah, the Writings and the Wisdom Literature
(most of what we would call the Old Testament today) for his bar
mitzvah, Zechariah has a large body of Scripture to draw upon as the
Holy Spirit inspires this prophetic response to God's graciousness.
This response, in what we have come to call Zechariah's *Benedictus*,
is a cascade of Old Testament thematic echoes and messianic
overtones that speak to the character, nature and purposes of God.
Zechariah was suddenly echoing the messianic tradition embodied
in his 500-year old prophetic name! ■

For "Reflections to Share, Journal and Ponder" see page 57.

11

Some Closing Thoughts

And the child grew and became strong in spirit; and he lived in the desert until he appeared publicly to Israel. (80)

As far as we know, Zechariah and Elizabeth never lived to see the "fullness of time" for their son John, who would become know as "the Baptist." They likely never experienced his ministry in preparing the way for Jesus the Messiah. Zechariah and Elizabeth most likely died sometime before John's adulthood, even perhaps during his formative years. If so, Zechariah and Elizabeth would never have seen the fullness of God's intended plan for their son, nor the impact he would have on the nation.

In the eyes of many, John became the *de facto* High Priest of Israel. His venue was the desert, not the Temple. His life and ministry were a protest against the corruption of the Temple leadership in Jerusalem. His protest against the Jerusalem establishment manifested itself in where he ministered, in what he wore and what he ate, as well as in the nature of his message of repentance. In God's plan, John was the one ordained to serve at Jesus' ordination-into-ministry "baptism" at the Jordan River.

Like Joseph in Pharaoh's Egypt,[46] Zechariah and Elizabeth were never able to see nor understand the full impact and significance of their lives in God's wondrous plan. While they both saw and experienced enough to be enormously grateful to God, the full implications and reason for their lives in God's hands awaited their arrival in Heaven. Only then would the culmination of their providential purpose be fully revealed to them.

In closing this "digging deeper" contextual understanding of Zechariah and Elizabeth's faith journey, it seems that some sort of benediction is in order. And so as you go forward in faith remembering the persistent faith of this couple:

May God grant you daily strength to walk blamelessly before Him while you wait.

May you wait expectantly, but without any sense of rigid expectations, for the gracious glimpses and sovereign surprises He has in His perfect plan for you.

May you live each day knowing your life is a case history being written by God's hand to glorify Him and encourage the faith of others.

May you become a practicing historian of your own life always remembering both who God is and what He has already done for you.

And may you never forget that "nothing is impossible with God."

Always remember Zechariah and Elizabeth's reality as you journey through life with your unfulfilled longings. It is one of God's many gifts to you from His Word to encourage you to faithfully and persistently wait in Him. ■

For "Reflections to Share, Journal and Ponder" see page 58.

12

Looking Ahead

As Luke closes his first chapter, the stage is now set for the prophetic birth of Jesus the Messiah in the basement where small animals are kept in a modest half-cave house in Bethlehem.[47] This is an even more familiar narrative that we think we know and understand. But, like in that of Zechariah and Elizabeth, this is another story that we have viewed through our westernized lenses and filters for so long that we miss the fullness of its intended message.

Contrary to what tradition has long presented to us, it wasn't an "inn" with a "no vacancy" sign that greeted Mary and Joseph when they first arrived in Bethlehem, and it wasn't a "stable" where Jesus was born. There were no cows and horses present to observe this humble birth; they were too big for the small basement. Furthermore, those shepherds really weren't the romanticized figures we have made them out to be. In fact they were despised by their culture. And glorious though this scene was in heaven's eyes, from the perspective of Joseph's family clan in Bethlehem, it was hardly so. In fact, for those aware that there had not yet been a wedding ceremony in Nazareth for Mary and Joseph, the situation was downright offensive, surrounded with the shame of adultery.

Context suggests that a motif of shame encompasses the birth, death and life of Jesus the Messiah. From a first-century Bethlehem mindset, it appears that Jesus was most likely born in culturally perceived shame. Luke tells us His birth was first announced to shepherds who earned a subsistence living practicing a shameful profession. Then at the end of His earthly ministry, Jesus died on a shameful Roman cross.

Furthermore, for much of His ministry, Jesus lifted people out of the shame and "sinner" status that their religious culture had imposed upon them because of their deformities, diseases, social condition or "unclean" professions. In rescuing these marginalized "outsiders" from their social prisons of guilt and shame, Jesus gave them a hope and a future they never thought possible. As He did so, He also invited them to join with Him in establishing a new community of salvation—The Kingdom of God. For these people, forced into cultural shame, and mired in it with no hope of ever being freed from its consequences, this truly was astonishing "Good News!"

By now, you have the idea: the full message of even the most well known of Bible events is rooted in the original context that surrounds it. Rebuilding that context allows us to better understand what really happened during those extraordinary days, and therefore to delve more deeply into what Luke intended his narrative to reveal to us. As a famous newscaster would say, when it comes to the Christmas account of the birth of Jesus, what we need is "the rest of the story." Only then will we be able to praise God even more, not just for what He did at Bethlehem, but also for the intentional way that He eternally chose to do it.

As enticing as it is to now dive into Luke's second chapter, the fullness and richness of that narrative is best saved for another day. ■

Reflections
TO SHARE, JOURNAL AND PONDER

1 A Priest is Born

Any Bible concordance suggests that "remembering" is one of the prevalent themes of the Scriptures. It seems as if the Lord is continually reminding us to remember who *I am* and what I do and have done for you because of who *I am*. It is natural to ask: Why these frequent reminders to remember? The answer is that God, knowing humanity perfectly, knows how quickly and how easily we tend to forget. Since a strong and vital faith is built on constantly remembering both God's nature and His deeds, neglecting the discipline of remembering deprives us of much faith-sustaining encouragement. Since our past is littered with signposts of God's enduring faithfulness to us, we need to be people who always remember never to forget!

■ How did your name come to be? Does it have lasting significance to you, to your family, to others?

■ If you could rename yourself with a more meaningful name, what name(s) might you chose?

■ The purpose of naming in first century culture often was to encourage the name-bearer to remember something about God and what He has done. Since most of our contemporary names were not chosen for that purpose, how do you best remind yourself of who God is—His character, nature and attributes—and what He has done for you because of who He is?

■ Hopeful events often occur in dark times. Has God given you encouraging, even joyful experiences during your dark times?

Ponder

I will remember the deeds of the Lord: yes, I will remember your miracles of long ago. I will meditate on all your works and consider all your mighty deeds. Psalm 77:11&12

On my bed I remember you; I think of you through the watches of the night. Psalm 63:6

2 Great Expectations

Often when we set our expectations, we also set the stage for our disappointments. Life seldom turns out like we thought or hoped it would. Thus we need to be people who hold our hopes and dreams loosely, not clutching them as if there is only one way they can be.

God is faithful, yet very unpredictable. As a result, we can comprehend only a small portion of what God is really doing in and with our lives. Thus we need to be people who are fostering a sense of expectancy, while at the same time avoiding rigid expectations of how and when God should be doing things in and with our lives.

- Has a parent, teacher or a friend ever projected (very) high hopes upon you? Expectations so high that you felt you couldn't possibly ever measure up? That you would never be good enough? How did that affect you? How is that still affecting you?

- Have you ever had situations and experiences in which, by the very process of defining your expectations you also planted the seeds of your disappointments?

- How can we best live with a continual sense of expectancy, totally trusting in God's providence and timing, without slipping into any sense of rigid expectations of how and when He should do things for us?

- Does it seem to you that you started out on a life journey where the early stages seemed to unfold in pleasant, even satisfying ways? But then you slowly drifted into a detour, then a cul de sac, or maybe even a dead end? What did that realization do to you as you experienced these changes in your life's hoped-for plan? How did that affect your time with God, your view of God, and your desire to be faithful?

Ponder

In the morning, O Lord, you hear my voice; in the morning I lay my requests before you and wait in expectation. Psalm 5:3

In his heart a man plans his course, but the Lord determines his steps.
Proverbs 16:9

Many are the plans in a man's heart, but it is the Lord's purpose that prevails. Proverbs 19:21

3 Waiting

An early theme in Luke is one of waiting with "unfulfilled longings." The nation of Israel is waiting for Messiah to come to the "Promised Land" and overthrow Roman rule, bringing a new spirit to Temple leadership. Zechariah and Elizabeth continue to wait for a child. Later in Luke's second chapter, we encounter Simeon and Anna, both of whom have been waiting on the Lord for decades in the Temple courts.

In Luke's narrative, waiting is both a foundational motif of Advent as well as an essential thread in the fabric of faith. Like Zechariah and Elizabeth, we have all had significant periods of waiting in our lives. With our culture evermore focused on instant gratification, fostered in part by our microwave technology and fast-track expectations, we seem to have become a people who find it more and more difficult to wait.

- Do you have predetermined views of how and when God is supposed to do things for you? Do you have your own notions of how God's blessing system should work?

- Have you ever had experiences of "waiting on the Lord?" Waiting for Him to do something that seemed so right? How about waiting for so long that it seemed you were waiting in vain? What are or were you waiting for? How did that waiting affect you?

- Have you ever had to wait on the Lord during periods of illness, unemployment, singleness, wayward children, infertility, or spiritual dryness? For how long? What challenges, encouragements, affirmations, discouragements, did you experience during those times of prolonged waiting?

- What is the hardest thing for you when it comes to waiting on the Lord?

■ Have you had any waiting disappointments that caused you to feel that somehow God short-changed you in life? When? Why?

■ Like Zechariah, have you ever felt like you were standing alone in some collegial circle? Or maybe that you were an odd duck in a family setting? What was it like for you? What did it do to you?

■ What happens to us when something comes along that doesn't fit our timetable expectations? Like Zechariah and Elizabeth's religious culture, do we compound the situation by the way we may inappropriately respond to it, or reinterpret the facts to fit our preconceived ideas?

■ In what ways do our views of how God should bless us shape or change the nature of our contentment? Do they erode our ability to confidently rest in His all-sufficiency for all aspects of our lives?

Ponder

Wait for the Lord; be strong and take heart and wait for the Lord.
Psalm 27:14

I wait for the Lord, my soul waits, and in his word I put my hope. My soul waits for the Lord, more than watchmen wait for the morning.
Psalm 130:5&6a

Trust in the Lord with all your heart and lean not on your own understanding; in all your ways acknowledge him, and he will make your paths straight. Proverbs 3:5&6

4 Being Misunderstood

Is there something at this point in Zechariah and Elizabeth's journey that strikes you as unfair? Are your instincts telling you that good and faithful people deserve more than this from God? Have you ever found yourself applying that same logic to your own life? Since you have been "good" for a time or a season, you therefore deserve something (more) from God? Such thinking does raise the question of who defines what's fair—the Creator or the created? If you or I deserved something from God, would it be His grace that provides it to us, or our own effort? It also raises the whole issue of our view of God and whether it is an accurate view, or a self-created, self-serving one.

Luke uses this couple to show us what it means to be faithful, even when life just doesn't seem to go in the direction(s) we thought or hoped it would. They show us how to remain faithful even when our unfulfilled longings seem to dictate there is no longer any reason to do so. This couple not only prayed during all these emotional seasons, but continued to honor God's commandments and requirements, and with a heart that pleased God. For Zechariah and Elizabeth, faith was a verb they lived out every day, every year, every decade, no matter what. In giving us these glimpses into their lives, Luke reminds us that God does not guarantee us an easy road or a light burden in life.

A friend of our family long ago observed that there is no greater burden than being misunderstood and realizing there is nothing you can do about it. Zechariah and Elizabeth lived with that reality every day for more than thirty years.

Isn't it amazing how even a religious culture, supposedly focused on God's Word and God's ways, can still misrepresent God's heart of mercy and inflict pain on His people?

■ Like Elizabeth, have you ever had a time when your sense of identity and purpose seemed to be at risk of being negated or unfulfilled?

■ Have you ever been painfully misunderstood in your religious or social culture and realized there was nothing you could do about it?

■ Why is it that it seems as if our deepest wounds come not from the world, but from the church? Is it inevitable that righteous people will be always wounded by their "religious" culture?

■ Have you ever been wounded by a religious community? What did that do to you? Have you ever similarly wounded others? How did you deal with that when you became aware of it?

■ What emotional reality most touched you in this section? Is there some part of your emotional past that the Holy Spirit still needs to touch, release, restore, and set free? Spend time in prayer, solitude, silence, meditation and contemplation asking the Holy Spirit to lead you into those areas of your life that are still constrained. As led, ask Jesus to set you free and restore you in those area(s).

Ponder

My friends and companions avoid me because of my wounds; my neighbors stay far away. Psalm 38:11

When my spirit grows faint within me, it is you who know my way. Psalm 142:3

Delight yourself in the Lord and he will give you the desires of your heart. Commit your way to the Lord; trust in him and he will do this: He will make your righteousness shine like the dawn, the justice of your cause like the noonday sun. Be still before the Lord and wait patiently for him. Psalm 37:4–7

5 Unfulfilled Longings and God's Plan

With the deliberate choice of the present-tense verb, "walking," Luke tells us what to do when our unfulfilled longings are unrealized. Like Zechariah and Elizabeth, we should simply persist in continuing to be faithful and obedient, even when all hope for what we wait for appears to be gone.

Given the pressures of his religious culture, it took great courage for Zechariah to continue to accept Elizabeth's barrenness. Given the importance of childbearing, it would have been perfectly acceptable for Zechariah after a decade or so to either divorce Elizabeth and remarry, or to take multiple wives. Indicative of this mindset, some rabbis taught that after ten years of childlessness a man was mandated to take a second wife.[48] Had Zechariah elected to take such an approach to solving his dilemma, his religious culture would have commended him. He would have been viewed as making a reasonable, rational decision to enhance his self-interests. Then again, maybe Zechariah somehow knew that the ways condoned by his religious culture were not necessarily options for him, that God had a different call upon his life. Perhaps he took time to remember the late-in-life births experienced by Abraham and Sarah[49], and Samuel's mother Hannah ("and the Lord remembered her"[50]) and recalling their faith journeys strengthened him to be able to wait some more.

- Can you relate to Zechariah and Elizabeth's decades-long sense of unfulfilled longings? Is there anything in your life that you would consider to be an unfulfilled longing? Was it, or is it hard to share that with others?

- If you were Zechariah, would you have stayed married only to Elizabeth after ten years?

- Have you ever had to deal with chronic issues of rejection or humiliation day after day, year after year, decade after decade? What did that do to you? How did you adjust to living with them?

- Looking back in the "rear view mirror" of your life, can you see where God's hand was at work, even when you didn't know it and couldn't see it.

- Have you ever thought about thanking God for what He has already prepared for the rest of your life? Those perfect plans of His that have yet to unfold of which you are not even aware?

Ponder

My soul is in anguish. How long, O Lord, how long? Psalm 6:3

All my longings lie open before you, O Lord; my sighing is not hidden from you. Psalm 38:9

Cast your cares on the Lord and he will sustain you. Psalm 55:22

But as for me, I will always have hope; I will praise you more and more. Psalm 71:14

But those who hope in the Lord will renew their strength. They will soar on wings of eagles; they will run and not grow weary, they will walk and not be faint. Isaiah 40:31

6 Dashed Dreams

The quality of our waiting says much about our faith as well as our view of God. It also speaks to our understanding and confidence in who God is, and our ability to fully trust in His will and His ways.

From where did Zechariah and Elizabeth's capacity to persevere in faithfully persisting come? Like all things, it was a gift from God. It was His gracious provision to sustain this couple during their times of prolonged waiting until His "fullness of time" had come for them. Later, Paul would remind the Corinthians of this spiritual reality when he asked them, "What do you have that you did not receive?"[51]

■ Have you ever had to face a point of no return in some aspect of your life when all hope seemed to be gone? What was that like for you? How did that affect your relationship with God?

■ Did you consciously ever have the sense that God was giving you an extra measure of faith during long waiting seasons of your life?

■ Is your time with God dependent upon your life's circumstances or your expectations of God?

■ Have you had times in your life when it was particularly challenging to faithfully wait, and to do so with a right heart? Can you relate to four decades of persistently waiting that way?

■ So far, what do you most admire about Zechariah and Elizabeth? How would you most like to emulate them in your own life?

Ponder

He will have no fear of bad news: his heart is steadfast, trusting in the Lord. Psalm 112:7

The Lord is close to the brokenhearted and saves those who are crushed in spirit. Psalm 34:18

My soul finds rest in God alone; my salvation comes from him. He alone is my rock and my salvation; he is my fortress, I will never be shaken. Psalm 62:1&2

Those who sow in tears will reap with songs of joy. He who goes out weeping, carrying seeds to sow, will return with songs of joy, carrying sheaves with him. Psalm 126:5&6

7 An Incredible Announcement

Luke shows us in this narrative that there can be long periods of time between the initial expression of the prayers of our heart, our prolonged periods of "waiting," and God's surprising ways. God's long-term plan is to remake our character and reveal His glory. Yet our short-term desire is often for immediate gratification and prompt removal of trying circumstances. Obviously, these are two very different and conflicting objectives! Luke also tells us something about God's nature and His ways in this story. We see a God who is utterly faithful yet, at the same time, totally unpredictable in his reliability!

We also learn from Luke's narrative that God sometimes uses enforced periods of silence, both for our benefit and His glory. Often He does this to get our attention (again). Frequently it seems as if His purpose is to interrupt our preoccupation with the trinkets and pursuits of this world. That way He can draw us to Himself once again, so that we can more clearly hear His voice to realize afresh and anew that we truly are His beloved.

- If you had been Zechariah, how would you have felt when you were finally selected through the lot-casting process?

- Can you relate to Zechariah's state of hearing but not really listening? Being so preoccupied that you miss much of what's actually being said?

- God's time frame and Zechariah's time frame of possibilities are certainly not the same. Can you relate to that from your personal experience? Can we totally trust God and rest in the fact that His timing is perfect while our notions of time are not?

- Have you ever felt that you have waited too long, or were waiting in vain? Felt that time, history, and maybe even God, had passed you by? Did those experiences allow you to imagine what might have been going through Zechariah's mind when he heard this sudden, surprising announcement?

- Has intentional solitude and silence been a part of your life? Do you set aside time to attentively listen to God's "still small voice?"

- Someone once observed that the word "illness" is totally contained within the word "stillness." What insights might that suggest? Have you ever experienced how God can take a time of "illness" in your life and redeem it into a time of "stillness" with Him? How about a period of prolonged unemployment? What was God teaching you during those times? What did you learn about listening? Where do you need to grow in learning to listen?

- Have you ever experienced a time of God's "imposed silence?" Was it an opportunity to refocus and be still before Him? What was God revealing to you during that time?

Ponder

The lot is cast into the lap, but its every decision is from the Lord. Proverbs 16:33

As the heavens are higher than the earth, so are my ways higher than your ways and my thoughts than your thoughts. Isaiah 55:9

Be still and know that I am God. Psalm 46:10a

8 Restoration

Over the course of his Gospel, Luke further develops this theme of sudden reversals that he initiates with Elizabeth's sudden restoration. This will become a major motif in his account of the ministry of Jesus. Luke will document Jesus' miraculous way of rescuing (saving) and restoring (lifting up) people by living out Isaiah's prophecy.[52] Jesus reiterates this prophecy in His "Nazareth Rescue Manifesto[53]", declaring that He will "proclaim freedom for the prisoners." Luke will repeatedly show us that Jesus did not merely heal people, but in doing so always restored them socially, spiritually and physically. Typical examples include the woman with the issue of blood,[54] the raising of the widow of Nain's son,[55] and reclamation of the Gergesene Demoniac.[56]

- How many times has God rescued you? Which was the most dramatic? Which was the most surprising?

- Have you ever been marginalized, only to experience God's restoration in unexpected ways? Can you relate to the Lord's rescue always leading to restoration? Have you experienced that progression in your own life?

- When you pray for others, do you put the emphasis of your prayers on their need for immediate rescue, or on their ultimate need for longer-term restoration?

- Has "nothing is impossible with God" been a reality in your life? How has that worked itself out in your circumstances?

- Where do you best identify with Zechariah and Elizabeth at this point in their journey?

Ponder

You have turned my wailing into dancing; you removed my sackcloth and clothed me with joy, that my heart may sing to you and not be silent. O Lord my God, I will give you thanks forever. Psalm 30:11–12

How great is your goodness which you have stored up for those who fear you, which you bestow in the sight of men on those who take refuge in you. Psalm 31:19

Say to God, "How awesome are your deeds! So great your power." Psalm 66:3

Let them know that it is your hand, that you, O Lord have done it. Psalm 109:27

9 God's Gracious Glimpse

Advent is a story of two wombs. One never opened and one long since closed. It is also a story about God for whom "nothing is impossible."

- Have you ever experience a sudden, unexpected event and immediately knew your life would never be quite the same again?

How did that realization affect you? Did you have to go through phases and stages of acceptance?

■ How many unanswered "why" questions do you still have in your life?

■ Can we totally trust God and rest in the fact that His timing is perfect while our notions are not?

■ What do you think Elizabeth's "rearview mirror" glimpse into the great "why" question of her life did for her soul?

■ Has God ever encouraged you by giving you glimpses of grace into the rear view mirror of some of the major issues and events of your life?

■ Have you ever wondered about the pleasant surprises that still await you in God's Providence?

■ What case histories of others' faith journeys has God used to encourage and strengthen you?

■ Is faith a verb to you that submits to God's will and ways regardless of the consequences?

■ If you envisioned your faith journey with God as a case history being written to encourage others, would it change the way you approach and live out each day? To declare yourself a follower of Jesus Christ means that many people will be watching you very closely, and for long periods of time. As an old bumper sticker once said, "Your life today may be the only Bible some people read."

Ponder

Lord, you have assigned me my portion and my cup; The boundary lines have fallen for me in pleasant places; surely I have a delightful inheritance. Psalm 16:5&6

As for God, his way is perfect; the word of the Lord is flawless. He is a shield for all those who take refuge in him. Psalm 18:30

My mouth is filled with your praise, declaring your splendor all day long. Psalm 71:8

10 A New Priest is Born

With this outpouring of praise, Zechariah and Elizabeth exit Luke's narrative stage, never to be seen again. Yet the reality of their persistently faithful journey continues to challenge and inspire us. It reminds all followers of Jesus Christ to never forget that He faithfully remembers His promises and His people. Because of that spiritual reality, Zechariah and Elizabeth encourage us to faithfully persist in walking blamelessly day after day.

When we are misunderstood because we are committed to God's will and ways,

When our unfulfilled longings go unmet,

Even when things make no sense to us;

When it seems like time has passed us by,

And even when all hope seems to be gone, because:

Our God is a faithful and gracious God who remembers,

Our God's perfect ways are always higher and better than our ways and

Because "nothing is impossible with God."

■ When was the last time you burst forth in a profusion of praise to God? What prompted it?

■ If worship means to respond to God, how much of each day do you spend in worship?

■ Regarding God's grace in your life, do you feel overwhelmed by its presence, or do you feel it has been meager for substantial periods of time?

■ Often what our religious culture thinks is reasonable and rational, and therefore recommends to us, is not necessarily what God would have us do. Do you have any examples from your past that illustrate this?

■ Zechariah memorized Scripture and the Holy Spirit was able to draw upon that in Zechariah's profusion of praise. Does that have any implications for your meditating upon God's Word?

Ponder

From the fullness of his grace we have all received one blessing after another. John 1:16

Praise the Lord, O my soul; praise his holy name. Praise the Lord, O my soul; and forget not all his benefits—who forgives your sins and heals your diseases, who redeems your life from the pit and crowns you with love and compassion, who satisfies your desires with good things so that your youth is renewed like the eagles. Psalm 103:1–5

11 Some Closing Thoughts

There will come a time in glory when disciples of Jesus Christ will see the totality of their lives as they were lived out in God's hand. That will not only take our breath away, but will cause everything in our respective lives to now make perfect sense! It will be a time when all "why" questions will be completely and perfectly answered. Because of that alone, we will have enough in our store houses of gratitude to praise God forever. In fact, as a participant in Heaven's eternal praise service, we may find ourselves sitting in the same pew as Zechariah and Elizabeth. Then we will join with them in praising God forever for the full wonder, utter faithfulness and consummate providence He manifested in all of our lives.

- Have you ever thought that your awareness and understanding of the significance of your life in God's hand is only the tip of the iceberg? That most of the impact you will have had in the lives of others in God's plan is always below the surface, still awaiting its full future revelation to you?

- Have you ever thought about praising and thanking God for what He has already done in your life that you are totally unaware of?

- How has this journey through Zechariah and Elizabeth's life encouraged you? Has it changed you in any way?

- What do you think you will remember about Luke's story of Zechariah and Elizabeth years from now?

Ponder

"For I know the plans I have for you," declares the Lord, "plans to prosper you and not to harm you, plans to give you hope and a future." Jeremiah 29:11

All the days ordained for me were written in your book before one of them came to be. Psalm 139:16b

Appendix

Luke's Text: The "Short Story"

The Birth of John the Baptist Foretold

⁵ In the time of Herod king of Judea there was a priest named Zechariah, who belonged to the priestly division of Abijah; his wife Elizabeth was also a descendant of Aaron. ⁶ Both of them were upright in the sight of God, observing all the Lord's commandments and regulations blamelessly. ⁷ But they had no children, because Elizabeth was barren; and they were both well along in years.

⁸ Once when Zechariah's division was on duty and he was serving as priest before God, ⁹ he was chosen by lot, according to the custom of the priesthood, to go into the temple of the Lord and burn incense. ¹⁰ And when the time for the burning of incense came, all the assembled worshippers were praying outside.

¹¹ Then an angel of the Lord appeared to him, standing at the right side of the altar of incense. ¹² When Zechariah saw him, he was startled and was gripped with fear. ¹³ But the angel said to him: "Do not be afraid, Zechariah; your prayer has been heard. Your wife Elizabeth will bear you a son, and you are to give him the name John. ¹⁴ He will be a joy and delight to you, and many will rejoice because of his birth, ¹⁵ for he will be great in the sight of the Lord. He is never to take wine or other fermented drink, and he will be filled with the Holy Spirit even from birth.— ¹⁶ Many of the people of Israel will he bring back to the Lord their God. ¹⁷ And he will go on before the Lord, in the spirit and power of Elijah, to turn the hearts of the fathers to their children and the disobedient to the wisdom of the righteous—to make ready a people prepared for the Lord." ¹⁸ Zechariah asked the angel, "How can I be sure of this? I am an old man and my wife is well along in years."

¹⁹ The angel answered, "I am Gabriel. I stand in the presence of God, and I have been sent to speak to you and to tell you this good

news. 20 And now you will be silent and not able to speak until the day this happens, because you did not believe my words, which will come true at their proper time." 21 Meanwhile, the people were waiting for Zechariah and wondering why he stayed so long in the temple. 22 When he came out, he could not speak to them. They realized he had seen a vision in the temple, for he kept making signs to them but remained unable to speak. 23 When his time of service was completed, he returned home. 24 After this his wife Elizabeth became pregnant and for five months remained in seclusion. 25 "The Lord has done this for me," she said. "In these days he has shown his favor and taken away my disgrace among the people."

The Birth of Jesus Foretold

26 In the sixth month, God sent the angel Gabriel to Nazareth, a town in Galilee, 27 to a virgin pledged to be married to a man named Joseph, a descendant of David. The virgin's name was Mary. 28 The angel went to her and said, "Greetings, you who are highly favored! The Lord is with you."

29 Mary was greatly troubled at his words and wondered what kind of greeting this might be. 30 But the angel said to her, "Do not be afraid, Mary, you have found favor with God. 31 You will be with child and give birth to a son, and you are to give him the name Jesus. 32 He will be great and will be called the Son of the Most High. The Lord God will give him the throne of his father David, 33 and he will reign over the house of Jacob forever; his kingdom will never end." 34 "How will this be," Mary asked the angel, "since I am a virgin?"

35 The angel answered, "The Holy Spirit will come upon you, and the power of the Most High will overshadow you. So the holy one to be born will be called—the Son of God. 36 Even Elizabeth your relative is going to have a child in her old age, and she who was said to be barren is in her sixth month. 37 For nothing is impossible with God." 38 "I am the Lord's servant," Mary answered. "May it be to me as you have said." Then the angel left her.

Mary Visits Elizabeth

39 At that time Mary got ready and hurried to a town in the hill country of Judea, 40 where she entered Zechariah's home and greeted Elizabeth. 41 When Elizabeth heard Mary's greeting, the baby leaped in her womb, and Elizabeth was filled with the Holy Spirit. 42 In a loud voice she exclaimed: "Blessed are you among women, and blessed is the child you will bear! 43 But why am I so favored, that the mother of my Lord should come to me? 44 As soon as the sound of your greeting reached my ears, the baby in my womb leaped for joy. 45 Blessed is she who has believed that what the Lord has said to her will be accomplished!"

Mary's Song

46 And Mary said: "My soul glorifies the Lord 47 and my spirit rejoices in God my Savior, 48 for he has been mindful of the humble state of his servant. From now on all generations will call me blessed, 49 for the Mighty One has done great things for me— holy is his name. 50 His mercy extends to those who fear him, from generation to generation. 51 He has performed mighty deeds with his arm; he has scattered those who are proud in their inmost thoughts. 52 He has brought down rulers from their thrones but has lifted up the humble. 53 He has filled the hungry with good things but has sent the rich away empty. 54 He has helped his servant Israel, remembering to be merciful 55 to Abraham and his descendants forever, even as he said to our fathers." 56 Mary stayed with Elizabeth for about three months and then returned home.

The Birth of John the Baptist

57 When it was time for Elizabeth to have her baby, she gave birth to a son. 58 Her neighbors and relatives heard that the Lord had shown her great mercy, and they shared her joy. 59 On the eighth day they came to circumcise the child, and they were going to name him after his father Zechariah, 60 but his mother spoke up and said, "No! He is to be called John." 61 They said to her, "There is no one among your relatives who has that name." 62 Then they made signs to his father, to find out what he would like to name the child. 63 He asked for a writing tablet, and to everyone's astonishment

he wrote, "His name is John." ⁶⁴ Immediately his mouth was opened and his tongue was loosed, and he began to speak, praising God. ⁶⁵ The neighbors were all filled with awe, and throughout the hill country of Judea people were talking about all these things. ⁶⁶ Everyone who heard this wondered about it, asking, "What then is this child going to be?" For the Lord's hand was with him.

Zechariah's Song

⁶⁷ His father Zechariah was filled with the Holy Spirit and prophesied: ⁶⁸ "Praise be to the Lord, the God of Israel, because he has come and has redeemed his people. ⁶⁹ He has raised up a horn—of salvation for us in the house of his servant David ⁷⁰ (as he said through his holy prophets of long ago), ⁷¹ salvation from our enemies and from the hand of all who hate us— ⁷² to show mercy to our fathers and to remember his holy covenant, ⁷³ the oath he swore to our father Abraham: ⁷⁴ to rescue us from the hand of our enemies, and to enable us to serve him without fear ⁷⁵ in holiness and righteousness before him all our days. ⁷⁶ And you, my child, will be called a prophet of the Most High; for you will go on before the Lord to prepare the way for him, ⁷⁷ to give his people the knowledge of salvation through the forgiveness of their sins, ⁷⁸ because of the tender mercy of our God, by which the rising sun will come to us from heaven ⁷⁹ to shine on those living in darkness and in the shadow of death, to guide our feet into the path of peace." ⁸⁰ And the child grew and became strong in spirit; and he lived in the desert until he appeared publicly to Israel.

Personal Reasons

My dream began to take shape while I was playing college basketball in the Midwest. As it slowly came into focus, I began to envision having twin sons, both being power forwards who would play at their Dad's alma mater—the University of Michigan. My dream was not nearly as significant as Zechariah and Elizabeth's dream, but a dream nevertheless.

At about that same time, Nancy, my wife-to-be, was completing her degree in elementary education. As God would have it, she was placed in a classroom of Downs Syndrome children. That experience profoundly shaped her and gave rise to a new prayer in her life. That new petition went something like this: "Lord, you can do whatever you want with my life, but don't ever let me have a child with retardation. I just won't be able to handle that!"

Several years later, we married, and several years after that our first daughter, Mary, was born. Three years later David arrived on the scene. We named him David Douglas, just in case he had some basketball genes in his makeup. In a matter of weeks, I was already musing on what his future jump shot might look like.

Slowly, over the first years of his life, David's mental retardation, cerebral palsy, learning disabilities and some of what they now call Autism tendencies, emerged. By the time he was three, it was clear it would be quite some time before he would ever hold a basketball, let alone shoot and score.

While Nancy and I were in the midst of sorting all this out, we learned that another sibling was soon to arrive. In as much as caring for David was equivalent to caring for two youngsters, the thought of a third child seemed overwhelming. So, after Sarah was born, while my wife was still in the hospital recovering, a surgical procedure ensured there would be no more children. For me, an unexpected line was suddenly drawn in the sand. Modest though my basketball-playing-twin-son dream was, it was now officially over. Our family sibling history had been written, just not in the way I had hoped it would be. That experience, in a small way, helps me to identify with Zechariah's unfulfilled longings for a son who could follow in his footsteps.

Needless to say, our life continued to change dramatically with David's development. Entering the world of special needs and special education, we were now traveling on different roads and down different paths than we had ever expected. In our own way, we had embarked on a journey like that of Zechariah and Elizabeth.

Twenty years later, our oldest daughter, Mary, became engaged to a basketball player, a wonderful young man who was a power forward who had set the scoring record for his university. Then, seven years later, younger daughter Sarah likewise found a wonderful husband, who likewise was a forward and loved basketball! Three years after that, in early 2004, both of my newly acquired "sons" joined the same recreation league basketball team. That led to a moment in early 2004 when both of them were actually playing on the court together as David cheered them on from courtside.

Somehow, like Zechariah, I too failed to immediately grasp the full significance of this event. Several days later, I awoke one morning with a wonderful thought: decades since I had first dreamed those dreams, I had three sons, two of them forwards playing basketball together. While it wasn't on Michigan's Big Ten basketball court, that hardly mattered. It might as well have been the Olympics for me. My modest dream had been fulfilled—just not quite in the way I had envisioned it. And I hadn't even prayed for it, at least consciously. God is so good. He is so gracious. He has His ways and He has His time. So in a small way, I can relate to Zechariah and Elizabeth's journey and relate to their surprise and delight.

I wish I could say we were in church, but we were in a hot tub some thirty years later. (Since we were then living in Southern California, that's just what you do. We tried to dignify that indulgence by referring to it as our conversation tub.) That particular night we were reflecting on our past, trying our best to be responsible historians of our own lives. We had just reached a time where we could see the end of our corporate days. Because of that, we had very recently made a decision to move back to Washington, DC and become onsite grandparents.

As we were reflecting on the thirty-two years of our multi-corporation journey, we revisited in our memories the several states where we had lived. As we reflected on those various moves, we were trying to connect the dots of how one position led to another, one company experience built on another, the kind of thinking reprobate engineers lapse into from time to time. But we weren't having much success connecting those dots. There appeared to be no good rhyme or reason for how these jobs progressed, no matter how hard we tried to put some sort of connective spin on them. Then, suddenly we were given one of those gracious glimpses by the Lord, and allowed to look in the "rear view mirror" of our life together to see something we had never seen before. What opened up before us was a glimpse of a consistent pattern of God's faithfulness to which we had long been oblivious. It was one of those wondrous "Aha" moments in God's grace.

What God revealed to us that night was that there was indeed very little professional rationale to my five job changes that took us to five different parts of the country. But, and here is the "rear view mirror" part, it all had to do with our son David. What we saw (and it took our breath away) was that each of those moves had everything to do with what David needed in terms of required services for the next stage of his life. Those corporate relocations were what God used to move us around for David's developmental benefit. Well, can you imagine how that sudden realization caused our hearts to skip a beat or two! All of a sudden we sensed a wonder to God's providence and a marvel concerning His ways that we always knew was there but couldn't see it. Like Zechariah and Elizabeth, we now had a wider-angle lens to see the reality of it in our own journey in God's hand.

God cares tremendously for David. As part of His continuity of care, He used corporations, with their hiring and firing, to move us around for our son's sake. We were thinking in a three-dimensional matrix, and God was at work in an infinite-dimensional matrix. That realization under-girded our belief yet again that God knows, God will provide and God is always at work. God has His ways, even when we don't realize it, can't see it, or can't fathom it. That's foundational, because one of the great concerns we have as David's parents is what happens to him when we go to glory? Where will he live? Who will watch over him? How will he be cared for?

With this glimpse through the rear view mirror of our lives, we were strengthened (yet again) in our faith in God so we could continue to go forth on this special-needs journey, like Mary, not knowing or having all the answers. We had to be responsible and try to do everything we could to prepare for David's future, but at the same time we had to trust, pray and go forward in faith as if everything depends upon God—which of course it always does. So, in our own way, we can relate to Zechariah and Elizabeth's faith journey. God gave us another measure of faith that evening so we could keep on keeping on.

Now you know some of the reasons why I found Luke's opening story so compelling, and why I wanted to reflect upon and share Zechariah and Elizabeth's faith insights and implications with you.

Ponder

Many, O Lord my God, are the wonders you have done. The things planned for us no one can recount to you; were I to speak and tell of them, they would be too many to declare. Psalm 40:5

The Case for Context

A text without a context is a pretext for a proof text. unknown

A Diagnosis

Words in Scripture have precise meanings; they always have and always will. Unfortunately, 2000 years of a Western worldview, layered with 300 years of modernity thinking, have taken a toll.[57] This has caused us to increasingly become egocentric people who prefer analysis, categorization and "how to" answers when reading the Biblical record. We have also been conditioned to prefer simplistic answers to deep questions. The results are all too evident:

- Spiritual narcissism is increasingly becoming the malignant condition of the church. This causes us to approach Scripture as if it's all about me—my Jesus, my salvation, my gifts, my call, my ministry—rather than first and foremost about Him.

- We increasingly don't know how to read the Bible accurately, let alone understand the intended purpose and meaning of a passage.

- Unaware that we are often overly practicing existentialists, we tend to focus on what we think or guess a passage might mean rather than dig deeper to discern what the Holy Spirit intended it to mean.

- With our "sound byte" orientation to life, we are too often focused on trying to quickly discern the "principles" of a verse or text rather than its intended purpose and meaning as part of a greater whole.

- We have a distinct preference for quick, easy answers packaged in spoon-fed formulas with simple diagrams, e.g. three steps to humility, four steps to effective prayer, five principles of righteousness.

- We are much more comfortable with analysis, quantification and tearing things apart, yet the Bible is all about synthesis and integration. Thus, we can easily become so preoccupied with analyzing a leaf (verse) under the microscope, that we forget the leaf came from a tree (book), and the tree came from a forest (the entire Bible).

■ We take the theological facts we discover and put them into categorized cubbyholes. Having labeled them, we convince ourselves that we have now mastered them. However, being able to identify and list all the attributes of God does not necessarily mean we "know" God!

Far too often these westernized, modern tendencies are as true for the pulpit as they are for the pew. When taken together, they create an interpretation climate that is alien to the world of the Bible. Because of this twenty-first century mindset, much of what the Gospel writers assumed their Middle Eastern readers would contextually know and understand is beyond our comprehension. While we still have the words of their texts, much of their assumed context is gone. As a result, we often hear only part of a story and therefore penetrate only a part of its message.

This more expansive and integrated contextual development of Luke's brief description of Zechariah and Elizabeth is intended to help us appreciate the crucial role that context plays in opening up the intended message of a passage. It should be a "given" that if we are going to connect with the full meaning of a passage for today, we first have to know what it meant for those we meet in the Bible. To do that, we have to adopt their mindset. As a result, understanding context becomes essential for several reasons:

Words Have Meaning

Words have very precise meanings in Scripture. That's why the Biblical writers intentionally chose their words under the guidance of the Holy Spirit to communicate an intentional message. For the Gospels, insights[58] into these word meanings include the following:

■ Literary context of the words used including their literary form, linguistic meaning and their use in rabbinic teaching pedagogy

■ Historical context they were rooted in, including the intertestamental and Roman occupation periods, as well as Israel's own extensive history

■ Geographical context of the sites mentioned including their physical characteristics, topographical and climatic features, as well as the extreme geographical variations that exist in this very small land

- Religious context they were drawn from including the nature of the Temple, Sabbath worship, the Oral Tradition, rabbinic interpretive wisdom, Messianic themes and prophecy, as well as ceremonial feasts and ritual purifications

- Village context issues including Jewish social customs of mandatory hospitality and social reciprocity, as well as the reality of farming and fishing life

Such an integrated contextual approach allows us to get closer to what the Biblical writers intended to communicate about who God is and what God wants to reveal to us in these passages and encounters.

Context Enhances Connectedness

One of the issues that every Bible teacher struggles with is how best to get the hearers of a lesson or message to connect with the text. As pertains to Luke's story of Zechariah and Elizabeth, it is how to help the listeners relate to and identify with this couple as real people, with real issues, in a real culture that was not particularly hospitable to them. We hope this contextual restoration of Luke 1 illustrates how helpful context can be in seeing ways to appropriately connect the realities of their story to the realities of our faith journeys today.

Context Sets Needed Boundaries

One of the problems with many Bible messages today, so often crafted without the inherent constraints and illumination of context, is that a passage can easily be taken into metaphorical realms the biblical writers never intended. It can also be treated in allegorical ways that may actually violate the intent of the text. Carried over into small group Bible studies, this can easily slide into group thinking where we collectively listen to everyone's version of "what do you think it means?" and then vote on the best answer. This may be good representative democracy, but it hardly qualifies for correctly handling the word of truth!

Context Allows Meaning to Emerge

In our church cultures today, the presentation of truth, if and when it occurs, is often done without its inherent meaning and purpose being developed. If the full meaning of a passage is to be grasped, the context of the passage needs to be appropriately developed. Reconstructing the fully integrated context of a passage is like staining a fine piece of wood. This approach does not change or alter the nature of its truth (its inherent grain), but rather serves to draw out the inherent grain of the passage so that its meaning and purpose can be more readily understood. In this way, the revealed truth can be first seen, then internalized, and then lived out in the reality of every day.

Context Gets to the Heart of the Matter

When all the pieces of the Middle Eastern contextual setting of a passage are rewoven back together for our western mindsets, we see some things have not changed in 2,000 years. People then, and people now, still struggle with the relational issues of abandonment, humiliation and rejection. These are the timeless realities of the human condition. Integrated context allows these issues to be drawn out of the passage for all to see. In doing so, the narrative touches our hearts and connects us with the reality of both the text and our own life experience. Watching Jesus rescue and restore people back then is to understand His non-changing heart for us now as we struggle with the same issues. Contextually restoring these Gospel encounters reveals the timeless truths of Jesus to be relevant to all ages, all cultures and all worldviews— even post-moderns.

Context Provides Direction for the Appropriate Use of Imagination

Jesus used the technique of imaginative storytelling not only to reveal more about His Father, but to teach his disciples how to live, think, feel and act in the Kingdom of God. His imaginative use of stories allowed His listeners to remember His message together with its purpose and meaning. His parables were consummate stories, rich with imaginative treatments of everyday images, situations and occurrences. His use of his listeners' imaginations not only allowed them to connect with the story, but also allowed them to internalize and pass it along to others.

In today's environment, using the word "imagination" in some Christian settings leads to the risk of being misunderstood. Today the word can also suggest meanings of fantasy, unreal, make believe, which were not how Jesus used His imaginative stories to connect with His listener's lives. He used imagination to bring out both the truth and the meaning of what He was communicating. In opening up a passage, we need to restore the rightful use of imagination in bringing out the full meaning of God's truth in memorable and transforming ways for pulpit, pew and culture.

Context Provides a Necessary Safety Net for "Rightly Handling the Word of Truth" (RSV)

Contextually reconstructing a passage not only suggests appropriate imaginative ways to make the text come alive for people, but also paradoxically sets limits on where that imaginative treatment can go. With the integrated context in place, limits are set on where interpolation of the text can be taken and where speculation cannot. This treatment of Zechariah and Elizabeth attempts to illustrate the use of appropriate interpolative imagination to connect with its readers, but in ways faithful to the writer's intent as defined by the fuller context of the narrative.

Context Allows Us to See The Whole Picture

All too often in our church lifetime, we end up being given many theological and doctrinal factual ornaments, but seldom are we shown the tree upon which to hang them. It's as if we have been handed dozens of pieces to a puzzle, but have never seen what the finished picture on the top of the puzzle box looks like. I am convinced that the more we can reset a passage back into its original context, the more we will see the complete picture. Even in this brief passage focused on Zechariah and Elizabeth, we see a big-picture theme of God revealing Himself for who He is, His will and His ways. We can also clearly see one of Luke's contextual themes of "rescue always leading to restoration." Both themes might not be all that obvious without our taking an integrated contextual approach.

Context Facilitates Transformation

If transformation of heart and mind is our objective, then it follows that the closer we get to the Bible writer's inspired intended meaning of the text, the closer we get to the epicenter of the Holy Spirit's intended transformation. Restoring the integrated context of a passage moves us closer to that epicenter.

Observations

We know that context matters in everything we do, and in everything we know. Yet somehow we seem to so easily forget that notion when we come to the Scriptures. Why is this? How did this come to be?

Reflections to Journal and Share

In the Middle East, the community is always more important than the individual. In the Western world, it seems to be axiomatic that the individual is always more important than the community. Since the Bible was written with an assumed Middle Eastern context, what implications does even this one presupposition have for Western worldview people encountering and interpreting the Word of God?

Without being aware of it, how many ways might we be filtering the message of the Bible through our Western worldview perspectives? Then further massaging it so that it fits neatly within our framework of modernity thinking? And then recasting it so it fits nicely within our comfort zones? It is no wonder that sometimes we just don't "hear" or "see" what the biblical writers intended to communicate to us.

In closing, I hope that this summary of the role of context in opening up the Scriptures helps to illustrate:

- Why contextual restoration of the Biblical record is crucial

- How the intended purpose and meaning of a passage can be more clearly discerned and develop

- How context can paradoxically set boundaries in interpreting a passage, but at the same times expand our understanding of its meaning

- How story telling within the constraints of the context can pull out much of the meaning in ways that otherwise might not fully connect with the reality of people's lives

Ponder

Do your best to present yourself to God as one approved, a workman who does not need to be ashamed and who correctly handles the word of truth. II Tim 2:15

Notes and Sources

1 David Allen, Handout from The Eleuthera Institute, Arlington, VA. Dr. David Allen, a Christian psychotherapist and author of "*In Search of the Heart*" has developed what he calls the "Bermuda Triangle of the Soul." His clinical experience suggests that the three sides of his "Bermuda Triangle"—abandonment, rejection and humiliation—speak to the human condition of every person. The only question is to what degree. Contained within that emotional triangle are the issues of guilt and shame, in what Dr. Allen calls "The Hurt Trail."

2 Peter Connolly, "*The Holy Land*", Oxford University Press, Oxford, 1994 p. 29.

3 Joachim Jeremias, "*Jerusalem in the Time of Jesus*", Fortress Press, Philadelphia, 1984, p. 192.

4 II Samuel 7:4—16 with a special emphasis on verses 12—14.

5 Gesenius' "*Hebrew-Chaldee Lexicon to the Old Testament*", Eerdmans, Grand Rapids, Michigan, 1974, p. 245.

6 "*The NIV Study Bible*", Zondervan Corporation, Grand Rapids, Michigan, 1985, p. 1406.

7 Ibid.

8 Joachim Jeremias, "*Jerusalem in the Time of Jesus*", p. 214.

9 Exodus 6:23.

10 Gesenius' "*Hebrew-Chaldee Lexicon to the Old Testament*", p. 245.

11 Genesis 1:28b.

12 James C. Martin, "*The Gospels in Context*", self published, 2002, pp. 33 & 34.

13 Exodus 23:26; Deuteronomy 7:17; Psalm 113:9.

14 John Hastings, "*Dictionary of the New Testament*", Baker Book House, Grand Rapids, Michigan, 1973, p. 844.

15 John 9:2

16 James Orr, "*The International Standard Bible Encyclopaedia*", Volume I, Eerdmans Publishing, 1957, p. 406

17 John Hastings, "*Dictionary of the New Testament*", p. 845

18 Alfred Edersheim, "*The Temple*", Kregel Publications, Grand Rapids, Michigan, 1997, p.101.

19 Chaim Richman, "*The Holy Temple of Jerusalem*", The Temple Institute, Carta, Jerusalem, 1997, p. 20.

20 Ibid.

21 Leen & Kathleen Rittmeyer, "*The Ritual of the Temple in the Time of Christ*", Carta, Jerusalem, 2002, p. 16.

22 Alfred Edersheim, "*The Temple*", p. 112.

23 Alfred Edersheim, "*The Temple*", p. 115.

24 Leen and Kathleen Rittmeyer, "*The Ritual of the Temple in the Time of Christ*", p. 37.

25 Chaim Richman, "*The Holy Temple of Jerusalem*", p. 21.

26 Ibid.

27 Alfred Edersheim, "*The Life and Times of Jesus the Messiah*", MacDonald Publishing Company, undated, p. 66.

28 David Allen. See note 1.

29 John Hastings, "*Dictionary of the New Testament*", p. 844.

30 Alfred Edersheim, "*The Life and Times of Jesus the Messiah*", p. 226.

31 John 1:14a.

32 John 3:16.

33 I am indebted to Dr. Dane Gordon of Colgate-Rochester Divinity School who shared these Advent thoughts during an Adult Forum at Summerville Presbyterian Church in Rochester, New York in December of 1974.

34 Leen and Kathleen Rittmeyer, "*The Ritual of the Temple in the Time of Christ*", p. 24.

35 "*The Interpreter's Bible*", Volume 8, Abingdon Press, Nashville, 1952, p. 31.

36 Leviticus 10:1 & 2.

37 Malachi 4:6a.

38 Alfred Edersheim, "*The Temple*", p. 115.

39 Ibid.

40 John Hastings, "*Dictionary of the New Testament*", p. 845.

41 Luke 7:28.

42 James C. Martin, "*The Gospels in Context*", p. 50.

43 Joachim Jeremias, "*Jerusalem in the Time of Jesus*", p. 340.

44 Luke 1:46–55.

45 Joel Green, "*The New International Commentary on the New Testament: The Gospel of Luke*", Eerdmans, Grand Rapids, 1997 p. 74.

46 Genesis 50:22.

47 James C. Martin, "*The Gospels in Context*", pp. 42 & 43.

48 Joachim Jeremias, "*Jerusalem in the Time of Jesus*", p. 372.

49 Genesis 17:16 and 18:13–14.

50 I Sam. 1:19.

51 I Cor. 4:7.

52 Isaiah 61:1.

53 Luke 4:18.

54 Luke 8:48.

55 Luke 7:18.

56 Luke 8:36.

57 Brian D. McLaren, "*A New Kind of Christian*", Jossey-Bass, A Wiley Company, San Francisco, pp. 106, 116 & 120.

58 Preserving Bible Times Website. See "*Role of Context*" page in the "*About Us*" section of www.preservingbibletimes.org.

Other Resources

For helpful information, seminars, publications and DVD visual resources for understanding and teaching the Bible in context, contact:

Preserving Bible Times
P.O. Box 83357
Gaithersburg, MD 20883-3357

E-mail: info@preservingbibletimes.org

www.preservingbibletimes.org

About the Author

Doug Greenwold is a long time teacher of the Scriptures. He received his BS, MS and MBA degrees from the University of Michigan, where he also played basketball. For thirty-two years, Doug worked in general management and executive positions in Information Systems, Healthcare Services, and Life Sciences. He retired from the corporate world in 1999 to teach, speak, and work with non-profit ministries.

In 1978, Doug discovered he was called to teach the Scriptures, his true vocation. An ordained Elder in three denominations, Doug has been teaching the Bible, writing and leading retreats, speaking at conferences and workshops, for churches and para-church ministries ever since. In 1989, he first visited Israel on a study program and realized the importance of integrating the context of the land with the biblical texts. Since then he has been an avid student and teacher of the Bible in context.

Presently Doug is the Executive Director of Preserving Bible Times, a non-profit organization dedicated to preserving and presenting biblical truth through contextual restoration of the biblical record. Previously he was a Teaching Fellow at the C. S. Lewis Institute in Washington, DC. Doug is also a Teaching Director in Community Bible Study as well as a Christian educator in the Washington, DC area. For the past several years, he has been engaged in researching and teaching "Luke in Context" and sharing the fruits of that work in his teaching, speaking and writing.

Doug and his wife Nancy live in Rockville, Maryland near their three children and two grandchildren.

Suggested Small Group Format

Session One

- An Invitation
- Luke's Text: The "Short Story" (Appendix)
- A Priest is Born

Session Two

- Great Expectations
- Waiting

Session Three

- Being Misunderstood
- Unfulfilled Longings and God's Plan

Session Four

- Dashed Dreams
- An Incredible Announcement

Session Five

- Restoration
- God's Gracious Glimpse

Session Six

- A New Priest is Born
- Some Closing Thoughts

Session Seven

- Looking Ahead
- Personal Reasons *(Appendix)*
- The Case for Context *(Appendix)*

Appropriate Discussion Questions for each Session can be found in *"Reflections to Share, Journal and Ponder"* on pages 45 to 59.